# Pardon Me:
# A Story of Second Chances

By **Darryl Loveless**

# Dedication

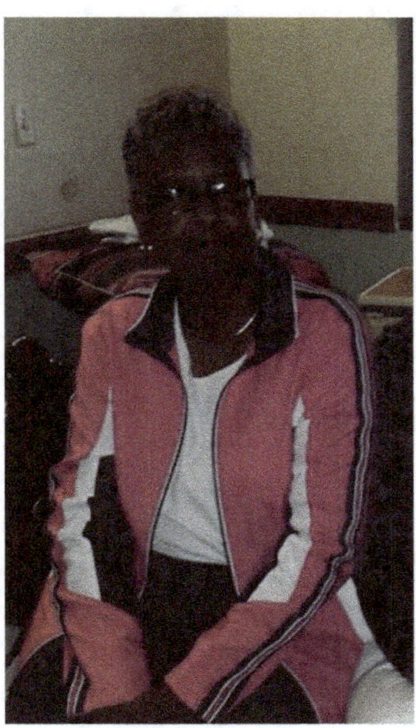

This book is dedicated to my mother, Ruby Stean Scott who always believed in me. Mom, thank you for allowing me to leave your nest at 17 years and 355 days. Thank you for not stopping me when I wanted to go outside the nest. Thank you for not giving me what I wanted but always having what I needed. Thank you for teaching me the importance of work and for always not accepting lacking in education.

You provided me with so much knowledge in just watching you. As a youngster, I thought you were just overprotecting me from being a man, and you were really teaching me to be a respectful, powerful, successful man. Look at us, moma, we did it! You and I, just like you said. I love you and cherish you.

# Table of Contents

# Chapter 1
# **The Bubble**

Let me take you back to the heart of a small, working-class African American community. It was the kind of place where everybody knew everybody, and our lives were like threads tightly woven together. Our house was nothing fancy—just four rooms to hold the stories and laughter of six people. A kitchen, two bedrooms, and a sitting room were all we had, but within those walls, our family shared a closeness that went beyond the limits of space. Our home, nestled between the familiar faces and narrow lanes, was a thread of stories that unfolded within the four walls holding the dreams of six souls.

In our about-sufficient home, my mom and I formed one part of the family, and my mom's older sister, Aunt Naomi, along with Uncle Walter and their two kids, Gwenetta and Victor, made up the other part. Victor, my cousin, and I were like peas in a pod. We were 7 months a part in age. People around the neighborhood often thought we were brothers because we were inseparable. We spent most of our day together and spilled all kinds of secrets. Our chemistry went beyond brotherhood. Despite our small living space, our home was filled with joy, warmth, and a strong sense of togetherness. The closeness broke all the limits of space and difficult economic conditions. Victor would later in life, join the Navy and spent 22 years in.

The small world outside the door was a buzzing hub of childhood adventures. Kids filled the streets with laughter and games, creating friendships that felt like family bonds. Most of our time was spent on the tight roads. Those streets had seen some of our best and worst sports performances. It was a time when the world was as big as our community, and every face was a familiar one.

As the seasons changed, so did the colors of our neighborhood. In the spring, vibrant blossoms painted the streets with hues of pink and lavender. The fragrance of flowers filled the air, and children played hopscotch and jumped rope on sidewalks marked with chalk drawings. Summer brought the sun down like a golden spotlight, turning the neighborhood into a lively playground. Kids raced down the streets on bicycles, their laughter merging. As the sun dipped below the horizon, games of hide-and-seek and tag continued under the soft glow of streetlights, a daily meet and greet that lingered long into the night.

Our neighborhood was more than just a collection of houses; it was a living, breathing entity. We might not have had fancy barbecues filled the air with the savory aroma of grilled meat where the sound of music drifted through open windows, or on special occasions, the community did not have much to come together for block parties, where tables groaned under the weight of potluck feasts, and everyone danced to the beats of local musicians. We did not have that kind of money, but our hearts were always fuller than our pockets – full of love and belonging.

In those times, my mom, a rock of wisdom, taught me the importance of hard work and saving money. After working in a rubber factory for 35 years, her hands, weathered by years of labor, told a silent tale of resilience. Lessons from her were not just words, but stories etched in the lines of her hands, shaping the way we saw the world. Her paycheck was not just a means to an end; it was a lifeline, carefully budgeted to stretch as far as possible. Every dollar earned was a small victory in the face of adversity, and every sacrifice made was with the singular goal of providing a brighter future for me.

She seemed to have perfectly balanced the roles of nurturer and breadwinner. The limited time we had together was filled with household chores, homework assistance, and the preparation of modest meals. All of this was to ensure that her love and care for me were never compromised, regardless of the time constraints.

Sundays were all about the church, where my mom's voice echoed in the choir. Her faith stood strong no matter how tough the times were. The church, with its welcoming doors and a congregation that felt like an extended family, was more than a place of worship for my mom. Her attendance was not merely a routine but a sacred commitment directing her life.

The values imparted by her religious beliefs permeated every aspect of her life. In the factory, amidst the hum of machinery, she carried herself with a grace that reflected the teachings of compassion, honesty, and hard work instilled by her faith. The challenges she faced were met not just with resilience but also with quiet trust in a higher purpose. It was a force that not only strengthened her resolve but should have also shaped my character to always be righteous. However, the reality was far from this.

As I entered my teenage years, my world expanded beyond our home. The excitement of revealing the unknown attracted me and gradually pushed me out, where new friendships, challenges, and lessons awaited. Sports became a big part of my life—football, baseball, basketball, and track and field. The playing fields weren't just where we competed; they were spaces where friendships grew deeper, victories were celebrated, and losses were faced together.

When I became more involved in sports, the companionship among teammates became a new source of friendship. The thrill of scoring a goal, making a winning shot, or crossing the finish line first became defining moments that brought not only personal accomplishment but also a sense of belonging to a team. The lessons of discipline, teamwork, and perseverance on the sports field were ones that went beyond the boundaries of the game, leaving a lasting imprint on my character.

Beyond the cheers and victories, I encountered the complexities of adolescence. The neighborhood that once felt like the entire world now seemed too small to contain my overflowing curiosity. Getting into trouble became an inevitable part of my journey. The same spirit that fueled my desire for exploration sometimes led me down paths that tested the boundaries set for an ambitious young boy. It wasn't rebellion for rebellion's sake; rather, it was the curiosity of a young man trying to understand the world around him.

Girls soon entered the equation, adding a new layer to my teenage adventures. The innocence of childhood crushes transformed into the complexities of teenage relationships. The first flutter of emotions, the awkwardness of shared glances, and the sweetness of holding hands became a rollercoaster of emotions that perfectly mirrored a teenager's struggle to stay on top of his game in all aspects of life.

Every relationship brought new emotions and lessons about love and navigating the tricky paths of the heart. Some memorable experiences also include being disliked by a dear girlfriend's mom and dad. There was not much to like about me at the time, especially for parents. Even though respectful, I was not engrossed in the safest activities, to say the least.

With my teenage years unfolding and my knowledge expanding with every interaction and experience, I was introduced to newer things. Smoking marijuana and sipping on beer seemed like a cool departure from the innocence of childhood, leading us into the uncharted territory of youthfulness.

The experiences of teenage rebellion whispered promises of excitement, and the attractiveness of marijuana became a temptation that led me into unsafe territories of enjoyment.

The haze of marijuana smoke became a cloud that enveloped me and my buddies. What started as casual experimentation evolved into a regular part of our teenage years. The once-clear lines of right and wrong blurred as the effects of marijuana offered a temporary escape from the challenges and uncertainties of growing up.

The company I kept, and my financial conditions played a significant role in shaping the trajectory of my teenage years. The influence of peers, each grappling with their own struggles and desires for independence, created an environment where experimentation with substances seemed like an inevitable part of growing up.

I had no idea of what life had in store for me as I escaped my little world, my bubble. If one had told me that my life would be worth writing about, I would not have believed them. But now there is no doubting the fact that how my stars aligned is a book-worthy story.

# Chapter 2
# **The Stray**

As I reached a crossroads in my late teenage years, the allure of the military encouraged me toward a different path than the college life many of my peers were pursuing. My best friend, Chris Marshall, and I went to see a recruiter and next thing you know, we both were in the Army. I just felt that the Army was a better move for me than being in college and my single mom taking care of me when I was old enough to do it myself.

So, after spending one semester at Alabama A&M University, I decided to drop out and join the Army. Immediately after basic training, I was sent to South Korea in the second infantry division, and our motto was Second Division second to none.

My first day there was an eye-opening one. The irony of racial discrimination being present in the military had just hit me.

My squad leader, Sgt Scruggs, greeted me. I had arrived after duty hours, so he did not have his uniform on. His outfit was a pair of jeans, cowboy boots, and a T-shirt, but the first thing I noticed was a big rebel belt buckle. Being from Alabama, I had seen that emblem a lot and never had any good experiences with it. He looked at me with disgust and ordered me to grab my bag, offering no help even after noticing I needed a hand carrying two duffle bags.

I was put in a room with two other white specialists who were upset that he put a private in the room with them. Soon after my roommates left, I was left all alone to unpack my bags to get myself situated for the next day of work when I heard a knock on my door.

On my door were soldiers who bunked across the hall. They went on and introduced themselves to me as Private Shook and Private Harsch and offered me a beer. They proceeded to tell me a little bit about the place, what to expect, where to eat and shower and then began to tell me to be careful around our squad leader because he was racist. That sounded strange coming from them. They proved to be a bit different than the white southern guys. Besides, Sgt. Scruggs was from Mississippi, so I knew what to expect from him. Private Shook told me that Sgt. Scruggs came to him and stated, "We now have a damn nigger in the squad." From then on, I understood that my race would be a bigger problem than I expected it to be.

However, the decision to join the military over college was a choice that would shape my character and bring me face to face with challenges and adventures I had never imagined.

The military, with its promise of discipline, adventure, and a sense of purpose, appealed to me in a way that college didn't. The team spirit and the prospect of becoming a tough, disciplined man drew me in. It was a decision that carried both excitement and a sense of duty—an opportunity to prove myself in a way that transcended the boundaries of my previous experiences.

With its demanding physical drills and mental challenges, basic training became a transformative journey for me. The military life molded me into a tougher version of myself. The early morning runs, the intense physical exercises, and the discipline instilled by drill sergeants became the building blocks of resilience that would serve me well in the years to come.

The military ethos of "adapt and overcome" became my mantra. The rigors of basic training taught me to face adversity head-on, pushing my limits and discovering strengths I never knew I had. The physical toughness I gained was matched by a mental capacity that allowed me to navigate the complexities of military life.

At 19 years old, I found myself settling into Army life in Korea—a journey that marked the beginning of a new chapter in my life. The unfamiliar sights, sounds, and tastes of a foreign land became the backdrop of my daily experiences. The diversity of faces and cultures within the military unit created a melting pot of shared stories and shared challenges.

Korea, with its vibrant traditions and rich history, offered me a perspective that went beyond the borders of my hometown. The experiences of adapting to a different culture, learning new customs, and forming connections with people from diverse backgrounds became integral parts of my personal growth. The military, which initially drew me in with promises of toughness, was now shaping me into a more open-minded and adaptable individual.

Army life in Korea was an experience filled with moments of friendship and shared struggles. The bonds formed with fellow soldiers, facing challenges together, became a source of strength and support. Whether navigating the intricacies of military drills or sharing stories during downtime, these connections created a sense of brotherhood that went beyond the duties of the uniform.

The responsibilities that came with Army life also brought a sense of purpose to me. The discipline instilled in me during basic training translated into a strong work ethic and a commitment to excellence in my duties. The skills I acquired were far from just military tactics; they encompassed leadership, teamwork, and a deep sense of responsibility toward my fellow soldiers.

As I navigated the complexities of Army life, the experiences in Korea shaped my character in profound ways. The toughness I gained was not just physical but extended into the resilience needed to face the uncertainties of military service. The exposure to diverse cultures broadened my perspective, fostering a sense of understanding.

The challenges of military life also meant sacrifices. The distance from family and the rigors of duty required me to dig deep into my newfound toughness. Letters and occasional phone calls became lifelines to the familiar world I left behind, providing a connection to my roots and a reminder of the reasons I chose this path.

The decision to join the, which initially seemed like a departure from the expected trajectory, became a transformative journey for me. It wasn't just about becoming a tough man; it was about embracing discipline and a sense of purpose that defined my early adult years. As I settled into Army life in Korea, the boy who once faced the haze of uncertainty and rebellion found clarity and direction in the structured, purpose-driven world of military service.

Late-night escapades became a sort of ritual for us soldiers. The vibrant pubs and lively nightlife of Korea provided a much-needed break from the rigid routines of military service. These were the moments where friendships were strengthened, stories were swapped, and laughter echoed through the night. The neon lights of the local pubs illuminated the bonds that grew stronger with each passing late-night revelry.

Amidst the fun, I struggled with the complexities of race within the ranks. The military, a microcosm of society, showcased both the promise of unity and the challenges of navigating racial dynamics. Days turned into discussions, and discussions turned into efforts to bridge the gaps. It wasn't just about toughness in physical drills but about emotional resilience, standing against prejudice, and fostering understanding among mates.

As time passed, my personal life took an unexpected turn. Love found its way into the barracks, and I fell for a fellow soldier—an incredible woman who shared my commitment to duty. Our love story unfolded regardless of the shared struggles of military life. We navigated late-night talks about our dreams, stolen glances during military functions, and the challenges of finding time for each other. The decision to get married marked a turning point in my military journey.

Being a husband in the military came with its own set of challenges and joys. The late-night conversations evolved into shared responsibilities, and stolen moments were part of our everyday lives. Love became the anchor that steadied us through the challenges of Army life. Together, we celebrated the victories, both big and small.

The biggest surprise came when we welcomed a baby boy into our lives. Fatherhood in the military meant juggling the responsibilities of a soldier with the joys and demands of raising a child. As time passed, letters and photographs from home became cherished lifelines, connecting me to the family I loved. The passage of time in the military took on a new meaning as I witnessed my son's milestones through letters and occasional phone calls.

As the seasons changed, so did the dynamics of Army life. The late-night parties, once a staple of our friends, evolved into moments of quiet reflection. The challenges of race within the ranks gradually transformed as mutual understanding and shared experiences bridged gaps. Love and family became sources of strength that resonated within the military community.

The passage of time in the military was marked not only by the ticking of the clock but also by the growth and transformation of individuals. The once uncertain young man, who had joined the Army seeking direction, found clarity and purpose in the structured yet unpredictable world of military service.

However, no one expected what was to follow. Life in the Army came with its own set of challenges, and financial struggles started creeping into my world. The command started pressuring me to fix things, warning me of serious consequences if I didn't sort out my money issues. It felt like a storm was brewing. Under this mounting pressure, I made a desperate decision that would eventually lead me into a world I never imagined—a world of crime. The constant struggle to make ends meet pushed me to consider something unthinkable. In a moment of desperation, I decided to transport drugs into the country, hoping it would bring financial relief.

A close friend told me that someone in the battalion was involved in a scheme that would allow me to make a quick 5k. It involved risk, but it had been tested, and it was bulletproof. He made the introduction and the plan was in motion. He told me to request leave as I was taking a 4-day trip locally. He then provided me with a false out-of-country leave approval and airfare to travel to Panama. He also provided me with a bag of clothes to give to his family members upon arrival in Panama. Unbeknown to me the bag contained over 100k dollars. I would find out when the person picked me up from the airport and took me to a hotel. Once in the hotel room, he started to rip apart the soles of the shoes that were in the bag I was carrying, and all of the money was concealed in there and rolled up in socks. I felt betrayed because no one told me that I was going to launder money.

So once the guy got me situated, he said I would be there for at least 2 days, and he pointed me to some eateries down the block. So, after getting unpacked and some unwinding, I decided to venture out on the block. The scene had totally changed from when I arrived. It was quiet and very little movement outside. Now it was dark, and everyone must have awakened. It looked like a carnival was going on. The streets were lit up, and partygoers were everywhere.

The streets of Panama felt unfamiliar as I went through with the plan. The weight of the briefcase seemed to symbolize the gravity of the choices I was making. I got the illegal cargo, slipped through the shadows, and managed to make it back without getting caught. The immediate financial relief provided a brief respite from the pressing money issues.

For a while, it seemed like my secret was safe. However, the consequences of that decision caught up with me three years later when someone else got caught, unraveling the conspiracy I had unknowingly become a part of.

The revelation hit hard. The legal implications of my actions became clear.

The military, an institution built on discipline and honor, now looked at me with suspicion. The financial struggles that led me to the crime were not an excuse in their eyes.

Chapter 3
# The Deed

Being in the military was one heck of a ride. When I enlisted, I didn't know what to expect. All I knew was that I wanted to serve my country and make a difference. Eight months into my 12-month tour, I found myself reflecting on the ups and downs, the challenges and triumphs that have shaped my experience.

One of the pivotal moments in my military career was the Battalion ARTEP, or Army Training and Evaluation Program. It was a big deal because it was my chance to prove myself and potentially earn a promotion to E4. The pressure was on, and I was ready to give it my all.

But things took an unexpected turn when I was assigned to a mission with Sgt. Scruggs. Now, Sgt. Scruggs was a character, to say the least. He had a reputation for being a bit of a troublemaker, but I never thought much of it until that mission.

The mission started off like any other, with a sense of excitement and anticipation in the air. But then, I learned that Scruggs and, another soldier assigned to our team, had gone AWOL and gotten themselves drunk in a nearby village. I couldn't believe it. Not only was it against military protocol, but it also put our mission at risk.

Despite this setback, the commander brushed it off like it was no big deal. I couldn't help but feel frustrated and disappointed. It was clear that Scruggs's actions were a reflection of his lack of discipline and respect for authority.

As if that wasn't enough, just a month later, Scruggs found himself in even more trouble. He was charged with stealing and assaulting a fellow soldier. It was the last straw. He was swiftly discharged from the Army, and I couldn't help but feel relieved.

Scrugg's behavior was toxic, spreading bigotry and hatred wherever he went. His removal from the military was a victory not just for our unit but for the Army as a whole. It was a reminder that there's no place for intolerance or misconduct in the military.

With Scrugg's gone, I was able to focus on my own journey. A month later, I received orders transferring me to Fort Lewis, Washington. It was a bittersweet moment, leaving behind the familiar faces and routines of my current assignment but also excited for the new opportunities and adventures that awaited me.

As I packed my bags and prepared for the next chapter, I couldn't help but feel grateful for the lessons I had learned and the friendships I had made along the way. The military isn't always easy, but it has taught me resilience, discipline, and the importance of standing up for what's right.

With my tour in Korea finally over, I began my new life in the Evergreen state, Fort Lewis, Washington. It was a fresh start with new friends, new leaders, and the love of my life. I met Lisa, a fellow service member who lived in the barracks next door. She always greeted me kindly, unlike the flashy women I was used to. I loved to go out and party, but with my finances on the decline, I couldn't afford it anymore.

Lisa was different. She didn't ask for much, inviting me for pizza and ice cream even when I couldn't afford it. Our relationship blossomed, and soon she was pregnant with our son, Cedric. But the reality of our financial situation hit hard. The military pay for privates wasn't enough to make ends meet, and bills started piling up.

The stress of our financial troubles didn't go unnoticed by the military command. My First Sergeant called me in for a meeting, warning me that if bill collectors kept calling his office, I'd be chaptered out of the Army. I felt lost, not knowing where to turn.

Desperate for a solution, a friend introduced me to Jimmy, a fellow soldier who had a way to make quick cash. He offered me a job that promised $5000, but I knew it wouldn't be legal. However, with bill collectors hounding me, I felt like I had no other choice.

The plan was simple yet risky. I'd take leave for a few days, fly to Panama, meet some people there, and bring back a briefcase containing something illegal. That something turned out to be 5 kg of cocaine base.

The trip to Panama was nerve-wracking, especially so soon after the invasion. Some of the people I dealt with weren't fond of Americans, making the situation even more tense. One of them made it clear he didn't like me, cursing at me in broken English and Spanish.

I hadn't fully grasped the danger of the situation. We had just invaded their country and ousted the dictator. The backlash from locals was something I hadn't considered.

Despite the risks, I completed the transaction and returned to the United States with the briefcase and the promised $5000. But the ordeal left me shaken, realizing the gravity of what I had done and the dangers I had exposed myself to.

As I returned to Fort Lewis, I couldn't shake the feeling of guilt and fear. I felt as if I had jeopardized not only my military career but also my safety and the safety of those around me. It was a harsh lesson learned and one I would never forget. It would catch up with me, but not for a while.

Chapter 4

# The Fall From Grace

Life was on the upswing. Coaching three sports, building a reputation, getting promoted to Sgt., and even being nominated for Soldier Athlete of the Year and Family Soldier of the Year—things couldn't have seemed better. I was riding high on the wave of success, even considering making a career out of my military service. But just as quickly as everything had fallen into place, it all came crashing down.

It was a seemingly ordinary afternoon when my Platoon Sergeant approached me with a troubled expression, asking me to report to headquarters. His reluctance to explain only added to my unease. We had always had a good relationship, so I pressed him for answers. Reluctantly, he revealed that two gentlemen from the Criminal Investigation Division were waiting to arrest me.

As I made my way to headquarters, I noticed the presence of a TV news crew, and the thought of the embarrassment it would bring to my family made my stomach churn. In a split-second decision, I diverted course and drove straight to the Criminal Investigation Division office, confronting them before they could orchestrate a public spectacle.

The investigators were furious at being denied the opportunity to parade me in front of the cameras. Hours passed as I sat in their office, answering questions and trying to make sense of the accusations being thrown my way. Finally, I requested a lawyer, and with that, they begrudgingly released me.

For the next year, I lived in a state of uncertainty, the looming shadow of impending charges casting a pall over every aspect of my life. The outbreak of the Desert Storm War provided a temporary distraction as I was deployed to support the mission, hoping against hope that the chaos of war would somehow sweep away the troubles awaiting me back home.

But it was not to be. Upon my return from Desert Storm, barely two weeks later, I was formally arrested and charged with drug trafficking and importation. The weight of the accusations hit me like a ton of bricks, threatening to crush me under their burden. Suddenly, the life I had worked so hard to build was crumbling around me, leaving me adrift in a sea of uncertainty.

I spent five agonizing days in a civilian jail, my mind racing with questions, doubts, and fears. How had it come to this? Where had I gone wrong? And perhaps most importantly, how would I ever clear my name and reclaim my life?

As I sat in that cold, lonely cell, I knew that this was only the beginning of a long journey—a journey that would test me in ways I had never imagined. But I was determined to face whatever lay ahead with courage and resilience, holding fast to the belief that tough times would eventually end. And so, with a heavy heart and a determined spirit, I awaited my fate, ready to confront whatever challenges lay ahead.

Chapter 5
# The Road to Redemption

When I got out on bail, my heart was heavy, and my mind was tangled in worry. I picked up the phone and called my mother. Tears streamed down my face as I poured out my troubles to her. She listened, her voice a comforting balm in the storm of my emotions. After our conversation, I reached out to my Aunt Naomi, my mother's oldest sister. We talked for hours, my tears flowing freely as I shared my fears and uncertainties with her.

Aunt Naomi, wise and supportive as always, suggested that we seek out a private lawyer instead of relying on a court-appointed one. She advised me to find the best legal representation I could afford. So, I began my search, determined to find someone who could defend me fiercely in court.

After researching tirelessly, I stumbled upon Steve Staurset, a lawyer with an impressive track record. During our initial consultation, his confidence and eagerness to take on my case assured me that he was the right choice. But there was a hurdle—I needed $15,000 upfront to secure his services. I didn't have that kind of money, and I felt lost.

That's when Aunt Naomi suggested I reach out to my father, whom I hadn't spoken to in years. It was a difficult conversation, especially considering his recent retirement as a sheriff deputy. But with Aunt Naomi's help, he agreed to cover the cost of my legal defense.

With Steve Staurset by my side, I began to understand the gravity of the situation. He outlined the challenges ahead and advised me on the best course of action for my trial. One piece of information he shared shook me to the core—the judge overseeing my case, Honorable Jack Tanner, had a reputation for being tough on African American males. The thought terrified me.

As my trial loomed closer, my cousin Collis, the father of the boys I had been coaching, returned from his tour in Korea. He came by to offer support and learn about the situation I was facing. I disclosed everything to him, including my concerns about Judge Tanner's biases.

Little did I know, Judge Tanner had encountered me before, through Collis' son, Dupree. When Dupree spoke in court about how I had positively impacted his life, Judge Tanner's demeanor softened. The flood of character witnesses and Dupree's emotional testimony swayed the judge's decision.

Instead of a harsh prison sentence, Judge Tanner offered me five years of probation, with the condition that I continue working with kids and being a positive role model. It was a second chance I vowed not to squander.

Over the next decade, I dedicated myself to fulfilling Judge Tanner's expectations. I poured my heart into mentoring and coaching, determined to make a positive impact on the lives of young people.

As the years passed, I grappled with the consequences of my felony conviction. Job applications became a minefield, each "yes" to the felony question seemingly closing another door. I felt the weight of my past mistakes bearing down on me, crushing my hopes and dreams.

But I refused to let despair consume me. I turned to research, seeking a way to break free from the chains of my past. My first victory came when Governor Warner of Virginia granted me the restoration of my voting rights. It was a glimmer of hope lighting the path to redemption.

Encouraged by this success, I set my sights on regaining my right to bear arms—a fundamental part of my identity as a country boy. Without the means to hire a lawyer, I tackled the challenge head-on, armed with determination and a stack of law books from the library.

When I stood before the judge, representing myself, he was astonished by the thoroughness of my petition. He praised my efforts and granted my request, restoring my gun rights for hunting purposes.

His words lingered in my mind—"maybe pursue a career in being a lawyer." It planted a seed of possibility, a whisper of a future I hadn't dared to imagine.

With each victory, I reclaimed a piece of myself, inching closer to the freedom I so desperately craved. But the road ahead was long, fraught with obstacles and uncertainty. Yet, I refused to be daunted.

Armed with determination and the unwavering support of my loved ones, I embarked on a journey of redemption—a journey to reclaim my life and rewrite my story.

# Chapter 6
# **The Way Forward**

As my life began to take shape again, the restoration of my voting and gun rights brought a sense of liberation I hadn't felt in years. With each form signed, and each restriction lifted, a weight was lifted off my shoulders. It felt like I was reclaiming a piece of myself that had been lost in the turmoil of my past.

Being able to coach again was like finding my purpose anew. Stepping onto the court, surrounded by eager young athletes, filled me with a sense of pride and fulfillment. I started small, coaching freshman boys' basketball. It was a humble beginning, but it opened doors I never thought possible. In my first season at the helm, we finished with a commendable record of 12 wins and 3 losses. The boys gave their all on the court, their determination and teamwork shining through in every game.

When the season drew to a close, the head coach approached me with an offer that took me by surprise—he wanted me to stay on as a full-time coach for another year. It was an opportunity I couldn't pass up, a chance to continue nurturing the talent of these young athletes and guiding them towards success.

But our victory didn't end on the court. Through the generosity of sponsors and friends, I was able to provide each member of the championship team with their own championship rings—a first for any freshman team in the district. It was a moment of pride and accomplishment, a tangible symbol of their hard work and dedication throughout the season.

Before long, I found myself offered a position as a varsity assistant coach for the boys' team. It was a step up, a chance to prove myself on a bigger stage. I threw myself into the role with passion and dedication, pouring my heart into every practice and game.

But life has a funny way of surprising us when we least expect it. An opportunity arose for me to apply for the position of varsity girls' basketball coach. It was a daunting prospect—switching from coaching boys to coaching girls. But something inside me whispered that this was my chance for growth, my chance to embrace something new.

Stepping onto the court as the varsity girls' basketball coach for the first time was a moment I'll never forget. The gym buzzed with anticipation as the girls warmed up, their eyes fixed on me with a mix of curiosity and determination.

I felt a rush of pride as I addressed the team, my voice steady despite the butterflies in my stomach. I spoke of teamwork, dedication, and the power of believing in oneself. As the girls nodded in understanding, I knew that I was exactly where I was meant to be.

Coaching girls brought its own set of challenges and rewards. Their passion and enthusiasm were infectious, and their determination was inspiring. I found myself pushing them harder, challenging them to reach new heights both on and off the court.

But it wasn't just about basketball. As their coach, I became a mentor, a confidant, and a guiding light in their lives. I listened to their struggles, their fears, and their dreams, and I offered them the support and encouragement they needed to succeed.

# Chapter 7
# **The Pursuit of Dreams**

As I made my way through my coaching career, I encountered many interesting people along the way. But none left quite the impression as Greg Crompton did. Our friendship blossomed on the sidelines of the basketball court, our children's shared passion for the game bridging the gap between our worlds.

Greg was a government worker stationed at the Navy Yard, and our conversations often turned to the topic of employment. He couldn't understand why I wasn't pursuing a career in the government, given my military background. I hesitated, unsure how to broach the topic of my past.

But Greg was persistent, his curiosity fueled by genuine concern for my future. When I finally confided in him about my felony conviction and the barriers it posed to government work, he was doubtful. He assured me that I had been misinformed and that a single felony didn't automatically disqualify me from obtaining a clearance.

His words struck a chord within me. With Greg's guidance, I focused on research, scouring the internet and poring over library books in search of answers. And what I discovered was nothing short of a revelation—I wasn't barred from government work as I had once believed.

Encouraged by this newfound knowledge, I took a bold step forward and applied for a contract position overseas, supporting operations in Afghanistan and Iraq. The role required a secret clearance, a hurdle I initially feared I couldn't overcome.

But fate had other plans. Despite my felony conviction, I was offered the job, pending a successful background investigation for the clearance. It was a moment of validation, a testament to how far I had come since my darkest days.

The road ahead was fraught with uncertainty, but I faced it head-on, determined to seize this opportunity with both hands. And when the call came from the FBI, summoning me for an interview as part of the clearance process, I knew it was my chance to prove myself.

Sitting across from the agent, I laid bare my past, my mistakes, and my journey of redemption. I spoke of the lessons I had learned, the person I had become, and the future I hoped to build. And to my astonishment, the agent listened, his gaze thoughtful and attentive.

In the end, he recommended that I be granted a secret security clearance—a decision that filled me with pride and gratitude. It was a turning point, a door swinging open to a world of possibilities I had once deemed out of reach.

But with this newfound opportunity came difficult choices. My wife and I spent countless hours weighing the pros and cons, grappling with the idea of me leaving behind my coaching career to embark on a new adventure overseas.

In the end, we made the decision together, knowing that it would mean putting my coaching dreams on hold for the next five years. It wasn't easy, saying goodbye to the court where I had found solace and purpose, but it was a sacrifice we were willing to make for the sake of our future.

And so, with a heavy heart and a sense of anticipation, I hopped on a journey into the unknown. For five years, I put my life on the line, navigating the complexities of war-torn countries and embracing the challenges that came my way.

It was a time of growth, of hardship, and of moments that tested my resolve. But through it all, I held onto the knowledge that I was making a difference, both on the battlefield and in the lives of those I left behind at home.

# Chapter 8
# The Pardon

Returning home after so many years away felt like stepping into a dream. The familiar sights and sounds of my hometown brought a sense of comfort that I hadn't realized I'd been missing. But beneath the surface, there was an undercurrent of uncertainty, a nagging doubt that threatened to overshadow my homecoming.

As I settled back into the rhythm of daily life, I couldn't shake the feeling of restlessness that gnawed at my insides. Coaching had been my passion, my calling, and the thought of being denied the opportunity to return to the court was like a punch to the gut.

But life has a funny way of throwing curveballs when you least expect it. Despite my hopes and dreams, the county I once called home had changed its policies, making it clear that individuals with felony convictions were no longer welcome in coaching positions. It was a bitter pill to swallow, a harsh reminder of the mistakes of my past that continued to haunt me.

With my dreams of coaching dashed, I found myself at a crossroads, unsure of which path to take next. But as the days turned into weeks and the weeks into months, one thing became clear—I couldn't let this setback define me. I had fought too hard and endured too much to let a single roadblock derail my journey.

And so, armed with nothing but determination and a burning desire for redemption, I set out on a new quest—a quest for a presidential pardon that would clear my name and open the door to a future filled with possibility.

It wasn't an easy decision. The road ahead was fraught with uncertainty, and the chances of success were slim. But I refused to let fear hold me back. If there was one thing I had learned over the years, it was that sometimes, you have to take a leap of faith and trust that the universe will catch you.

With that mindset, I threw myself into the daunting task of navigating the process of seeking a presidential pardon. I spent hours studying legal documents and precedents and reaching out to anyone who might be able to offer guidance or assistance.

The law firms I had reached out to were hesitant to take on my case, fearing that time was running out with a new president ready to take seat.

It was a setback, to be sure. But I refused to let it deter me. I carried out extensive research and filed the request for pardon myself without any help.

And then, just when I least expected it, the call came. It was from the Department of Justice, bearing news that would change my life forever—a presidential pardon from President Barack Obama himself, granted on his last docket before leaving office.

It was a moment of pure, unadulterated triumph—a testament to the power of perseverance, faith, and the belief that second chances are always within reach.

With the weight of my past lifted from my shoulders, I wasted no time in returning to the court where I belonged. Once again, I was doing what I loved—coaching basketball, shaping young minds, and making a difference in the lives of others.

Chapter 9

# The Lessons

As I reflect on the journey of my life, one lesson stands out above all others—never give up on your dreams, and never let a mistake define your character. It's a lesson I've learned the hard way, through trials and tribulations that tested my resolve and challenged my faith. But through it all, I've come to understand the true power of forgiveness and the importance of taking second chances.

Life is full of ups and downs, twists and turns that can leave us feeling lost and uncertain. But amidst the chaos and confusion, there is a guiding light—a beacon of hope that reminds us of the inherent goodness within us all. For God did not make us perfect beings; He made us flawed and fallible, capable of both great triumphs and devastating mistakes.

But it is in our imperfections that we find our humanity, our capacity for growth and redemption. For if we are willing to forgive others their trespasses, so too will we be forgiven. It's a simple yet profound truth that has the power to transform lives and heal wounded hearts.

Throughout my own journey, I've been blessed with countless second chances—opportunities to right the wrongs of my past and chart a new course for the future. And while the road hasn't always been easy, each setback has only served to strengthen my resolve and deepen my faith.

I've learned that true forgiveness is not just about letting go of the past; it's about embracing the present and the potential for a brighter tomorrow. It's about recognizing that we are all deserving of love and compassion, regardless of our mistakes or shortcomings.

And so, as I look back on the twists and turns of my own life, I am filled with gratitude for the second chances I've been given—the chance to coach again, the chance to seek redemption, and the chance to inspire others to do the same.

My message to you, dear reader, is simple yet profound: embrace second chances with an open heart and a willing spirit. For in doing so, you will not only find forgiveness for others but also for yourself. And in that forgiveness lies the key to true freedom and lasting peace.

So let go of the past, forgive those who have wronged you, and embrace the beauty of the present moment. For in the end, it is forgiveness that sets us free and allows us to live the life we were meant to live—a life filled with love, joy, and endless possibility.